The M

Cookbook

by Barbara Santos

CELESTIAL ARTS
BERKELEY, CA

CELESTIAL ARTS PUBLISHING
P.O. Box 7123
Berkeley, California 94707

Cover design: Marlene McLoghlin
Text design: Brad Greene

Printed in Singapore
Library of Congress Catalog Card Number: 96-83235

First Printing, 1996

1 2 3 4 / 99 98 97 96

TABLE OF CONTENTS

The Sweetest Onion

For me, it's hard to beat the aroma of onion cooking gently in a little olive oil. Onion provided the soul of Dad's stew, Mom's salads, Grandma's soup, and Auntie's spaghetti sauce. But my favorite onion dish of all back then was a slice of crisp raw onion, sprinkled with salt and pepper, between two pieces of white Wonder Bread. We regularly ran out of eggs or milk, but we always had an onion or two left in the net bag in the back of the pantry.

Somewhere along the way, the too-obliging onion became boring. Worse yet, it was socially unacceptable to risk onion breath on a date. "...hold the onion, please." Then I grew up, moved to Maui, and found an onion I could love...

Transcending the lowly reputation of the typical onion, the sweet Maui onion is developing a fan club of onion aficionados. Local food festivals now feature the famous rotund root. It is happily sliced and diced by top chefs who know its subtle character so well. Honored for its sheer beauty and size in agricultural shows, it even has its own event each August at

Whalers Village in Kaanapali—The Maui Onion Festival. Meanwhile, cooking contests have inspired hundreds of wonderful recipes over the past few years. *The Totally Maui Onion Cookbook* features the best recipes from the finest chefs competing at the most popular food festivals on the island.

Most of these recipes call for cooked onion but, remember, the Maui onion is wonderful raw and naked. In fact, that is the best way to appreciate its distinct flavor. The Kula Maui onion is being marketed as the sweetest onion of all—and sweet it is!

But the gentle nature of a good Maui onion is the real hook. If you loved raw onions in your youth but can't take the gastro-intestinal repercussions any longer, the Maui onion can offer that aromatic crunch without the odorous backlash. Loyal food enthusiasts will search out the extraordinary onion that grows only on the slopes of the dormant volcano, Haleakala.

Once impossibly rare and costly, Maui onions are now available almost year-round at reasonable prices. Visitors are able to take home as many Maui onions as they can stuff into their luggage—just as long as

The Sweetest Onion

the onion is declared and goes through the agricultural inspection at the airport with the rest of the souvenirs.

The Maui onion is a sweet mystery. What makes it such a mild and well-mannered vegetable? No one really knows for sure. But here are some theories:

Sunshine—People tend to think of Maui as a paradise of long sunny days. Wrong! Hawaiian days are surprisingly short when compared to the 'twilight until 9 p.m.' summer days on the Mainland. Hawaii is closer to the equator so Maui days are about 12 hours long year-round. Upcountry Maui also has a natural cloud cover that tempers the blazing sun. This keeps the onion from growing too quickly and allows plenty of time for the moisture and natural sugar levels to rise.

Altitude—The sweetest onions grown in Hawaii are planted on the slopes of Haleakala at 3,500 feet above the Pacific in an area called Kula, Maui. Temperatures hover here between 60 to 70 degrees F. Research done on Maui pineapples shows they can mature in about a year at sea level, but those grown up near Kula take 18 months to ripen. So, why do they still plant pineapple up the hill? It is the best and sweetest pineapple grown anywhere. Could there be a pineapple/onion correlation?

Rich, Red Earth—The volcanic soil may be yet another piece of the Maui onion puzzle. It's full of minerals, but Mauians know there is more to the earth, or *'aina*, than can be measured scientifically.

Total Maui farm acreage devoted to onions is less than a single mega-farm anywhere on the Mainland! Still, nearly 900 tons are grown in Maui County and much of it is being exported. Obviously, local farmers are experts at maximizing the yield while maintaining the land they cultivate.

Since 1993 the farmers and wholesalers (on Maui they are one and the same; The Maui Farmers Cooperative Exchange) have produced an ample and steady supply of Maui onion, certainly enough for exporting on a regular basis. Since its reputation has won many loyal customers, farmers are devoting even more acreage as the demand steadily increases. Watch for even wider availability and lower prices as huge tracts of abandoned sugar cane land becomes available. Distribution is under control now, as well. The Maui Produce Exchange in Pleasant Hills, California acts as the bulk distributor of the Maui onion.

The recipes in this book were created using Maui Kula Sweet onion which is the sweetest of the sweet. Vidalia, Walla Walla, or any sweet type of onion will give similar results. If you are using a more pungent variety, a speck of sugar added to most dishes will give the sweet taste that the Maui onion would have naturally provided. Don't be shy about allowing regional varieties of onion to impart their own essential quality to these recipes. But check your grocery store. Maui onion is probably available. No need to wait until your next trip to Maui. *Aloha...*

MAUI ONION PUPUS

Kihei Maui Onion Salsa

This salsa is ready to serve in minutes. We eat lots of it with corn chips after a day at the beach while the Maui burgers are grilling.

> 1 (14½-ounce) can stewed tomatoes, drained,
>   reserve the liquid
> 1 small Maui onion, quartered
> 1 small bunch fresh cilantro, leaves only
> 1 tablespoon Tiger Sauce or substitute
>   2 teaspoons sugar
> 1½ teaspoons Tabasco
> 1 package Portuguese sweet rolls or
>   similar bread

Put all ingredients, except reserved liquid, into food processor bowl. Pulse until onion is chopped into small bits. Pour equal amounts into two bowls. Mix enough reserved tomato liquid equally into the bowls until salsa is dipping consistency.

Hint: For both a mild and spicy version from one batch, put all the reserved liquid into just one bowl of salsa. This will be the 'mild' version. Label bowls.

Makes about 1 quart

Maui Onion Rice Paper Springrolls

Chef Martina Hilldorfer prepares the menu for the exquisite Sound of the Falls restaurant at the Westin Maui. Although it looks elegant when prepared, this recipe is surprisingly easy.

8 rice paper wrappers
8 jumbo shrimp, cooked
8 opal basil leaves
½ lime, juiced
1 carrot, julienned
8 lettuce leaves
1 small Maui onion, sliced
2 green onions, julienned
8 pieces fresh mint
2 ounces daikon sprouts or alfalfa sprouts
dipping sauce (recipe follows)

Soak rice paper in water until transparent. Divide ingredients equally onto each rice paper, keeping the fillings near the center. (Slice shrimp lengthwise, if desired.) Roll each rice paper like a burrito. Chill thoroughly. Serve with dipping sauce.

Makes 8 rolls

Dipping Sauce:

¼ cup rice wine vinegar
¼ cup sugar
Hawaiian chile peppers (small red) to taste
2 tablespoons crushed peanuts

Rule of thumb: The longer you cook a Maui onion, the sweeter it becomes.

Maui Onion Cold Canapé

Keeps in the refrigerator for about a month... if you can resist eating it all at once, according to its creator Paulette deMaestre.

6 to 8 large Maui onions
1 cup chopped celery
10 pimento-stuffed olives, cut in half
4 cloves garlic, preferably ground in mortar
    and pestle
3 tablespoons freshly chopped parsley
3 tablespoons minced capers
½ teaspoon oregano
½ teaspoon basil
1 teaspoon sugar
salt and freshly ground pepper to taste
1 (28-ounce) can Italian plum tomatoes,
    drained
¾ cup red wine vinegar with garlic
¾ cup pure virgin olive oil (half canola
    may be substituted)

Maui Onion Pupus

Cut Maui onions in eighths and sauté on low heat in very little olive oil until transparent but crunchy. In a large bowl stir together all other ingredients. Taste for seasoning. When onions are cool, add to bowl and mix well. Pour into two 1-quart glass jars, cover tightly and refrigerate. Use only wooden utensils to stir or remove from jar. Let marinate in refrigerator 24 to 36 hours before serving on toast rounds or crispy crackers.

Makes 2 quarts

Miniature Maui Onion Tarts

Charle Kenward owns Charle's House of Miniatures in Kihei. So it is especially appropriate that her recipe is made in miniature portions for pupus.

Crust:

2 cups all-purpose flour
1 teaspoon salt
$^2/_3$ cup shortening
2 tablespoons butter
4 to 5 tablespoons ice-cold water

Cut shortening and butter into flour and salt until pea-sized. Sprinkle with ice-cold water, 1 tablespoon at a time, fluff with a fork until you can press into a ball. Roll out dough and cut into 4-inch circles to line each cup in a muffin tin. Chill until ready to use.

Filling:

4 or 5 Maui onions, diced
½ cup water
1 cup sour cream (IMO for non-dairy)
½ teaspoon salt
¼ teaspoon pepper
2 tablespoons chopped fresh dill
2 tablespoons chopped fresh parsley
3 eggs, slightly beaten
1 egg white

Microwave onions in water about 3 minutes, or until transparent but still firm. Drain and cool. Heat sour cream, salt, pepper, chopped herbs and eggs for 2 minutes in microwave. Combine, then add drained onion. Brush the bottom of each tart crust with egg white and fill each with onion mixture.

Bake at 400 degrees F for 10 minutes and then reduce to 350 degrees F for another 15 minutes. Serve piping hot or cold. Can be made ahead and reheated.

Makes 12 tarts

Snookie's Maui Onion Mock Crab Cakes

Although this recipe has no crabmeat in it, Stephanie Ohigashi warns that the 'essence' in the soup mix may still bother anyone allergic to shellfish. So it is a poor man's crab cake but not an allergic man's crab cake!

2 cups Italian-style bread crumbs
1 (¼-ounce) envelope Maui onion soup mix
1 envelope Chinese-style seafood soup mix
   (crab flavor)*
2 eggs
1½ cups skim milk
¼ cup water
2 teaspoons Tabasco
2 teaspoons balsamic vinegar
2 teaspoons Maui Sweet Onion Mustard
1 Maui onion, quartered and sliced paper thin
½ cup cilantro, minced
½ cup carrots, shredded

* *available in Asian food section of grocery store*

Mix dry ingredients in large bowl. Beat eggs with milk, water, Tabasco, vinegar, and mustard. Add to dry mixture. Add vegetables and refrigerate for two hours. Shape into 1-inch balls, flatten and fry in pan with light coating of olive oil. Fry until golden brown on each side. Serve with guacamole or cocktail sauce.

Makes 36 mini-cakes

If you are using a pungent variety: Run a cup of water mixed with a tablespoon of vinegar over chopped onion in a strainer to take the 'bite' out of them.

Maui Onion Cheesecake...
as an Appetizer!

*Ginny and Dale Parsons worked with everyone from
Soupy Sales to Howard Stern before they left NBC
Radio in New York and moved to Maui. Radio is still a
big part of their lives...their son is even named D.J.!
This is an island twist on a Big Apple classic.*

    1 (5-ounce) package cream cheese
    2 cloves garlic
    1 egg
    1 (8-ounce) jar Maui onion jelly

Mix first three ingredients together with half the
jar of jelly. Pour mixture into greased, 6-inch
springform pan. Bake at 350 degrees F for 25 minutes. Cool completely and remove from pan. Heat
remaining jelly and pour over top of cheesecake.
Serve with a variety of crackers.

Maui Onion Tapanade

Joanna Jeronimo is an art critic for the Maui News.
While her backyard grill is working on the main course,
guests enjoy this easy, tasty appetizer.

> 1 large Maui onion, sliced into rings
> 1 cup stuffed green olives, rinsed
> 8 to 10 cloves of garlic
> 2 teaspoons fresh thyme
> 2 teaspoons fresh marjoram
> ½ teaspoon red pepper flakes
> dash of balsamic vinegar
> 1 teaspoon olive oil
> white pepper to taste

Grill onion and garlic. Place in food processor with
olives, herbs and red pepper flakes. Chop until well
blended. Add vinegar, drizzle olive oil and add white
pepper to taste. Process another 10 seconds then
place in serving dish and garnish. Toast slices of
dense bread on grill and serve with spread.

Makes about ¾ cup

Macadamia Nut-Crusted Brie with Maui Onion & Oven-Dried Tomato Relish

Chef Steve Amaral prefers to use fresh produce…so he turned a strip of the Kea Lani Hotel parking lot into an organic garden, incorporating fruit trees and herbs into the hotel landscaping.

4 small wheels of brie, cold
1 cup all-purpose flour
1 cup milk
3 eggs
1 cup finely chopped macadamia nuts
canola oil for frying

1 Maui onion, julienned
⅓ cup brown sugar
1 cup red wine vinegar
½ cup chicken stock
salt and pepper to taste
8 dried tomatoes
¼ cup capers

Brie:

Toss brie wheels in flour until well coated. Shake off excess flour. Beat milk and eggs together in a small bowl. Dip brie in egg mixture until well coated. Immediately dip brie in finely chopped macadamia nuts, patting with hands to 'set' the nuts. Heat oil in a pan deep enough to cover the cheese. Deep fry, or bake at 475 degrees F, until the cheese is golden brown.

Relish:

Brown Maui onions over medium heat. Stir in brown sugar. Cook until fully caramelized and glossy. Add chicken stock and vinegar. Season to taste with salt and pepper. Reduce on medium heat by two thirds. (Sauce will coat the back of a spoon.) Remove from heat and transfer to medium-sized bowl. Add dried tomatoes and capers. Cool, stirring occasionally. Sauce will thicken as it cools. Refrigerate. Relish will keep in the refrigerator up to two weeks.

Makes 4 wheels, one per person

Grilled Maui Onion Guacamole

Chef Roger Dikon uses the mellow taste of sweet onion to make this guacamole special.

1 large Maui onion
2 tablespoons olive oil
salt and pepper to taste
2 avocados, diced
1 large ripe tomato, diced
1 clove garlic, minced
2 tablespoons cilantro, chopped
2 tablespoons fresh lemon juice
juice of 1 lime
cayenne pepper to taste

Slice the onion into ¼-inch thick slices. Pour the olive oil and salt over the onions. Let sit for 30 minutes. Grill onion for 2 minutes, then set aside. Combine the rest of the ingredients in a bowl. Dice the onion and mix it into the guacamole. Serve at room temperature.

Serves 4

SWEET ONION SALADS

Maui Onion, Tomato & Mozzarella Slices with Capers & Basil

Just slice and assemble with fresh cheese from the Cassanova Deli in Makawao and vine-ripened tomato. To get the same chewy consistency with commercial mozzarella, however, you must microwave.

1 large Maui onion, sliced
1 large ripe tomato, sliced
1 pound mozzarella cheese ball, sliced
8 large whole basil leaves
1 tablespoon balsamic vinegar
1 tablespoon olive oil
2 tablespoons capers

Arrange sliced onion, tomato and cheese, slightly overlapping, in a circle on a microwave oven-proof plate. Place in microwave for 1 minute on high, until cheese just begins to soften.

Slice half of the basil leaves into thin strips and sprinkle over the plate. Drizzle vinegar and oil over all. Return to oven for 1 minute, or until cheese begins to melt.

Sprinkle capers and arrange remaining whole basil leaves in the middle of plate. Serve warm with sliced baguette.

Serves 4 as an appetizer

Snorkel Bob's Caesar Salad with Maui Onion

The Snorkel One suggests this be served immediately after tossing the greens. It's a meal in itself.

    1 head romaine lettuce, washed, dried and
        torn into large bite-sized pieces
    4 anchovies
    2 cloves of garlic
    1 tablespoon dry mustard powder
    dash black pepper
    juice from 1 lemon
    ¾ cup olive oil
    1 tablespoon Worcestershire sauce
    ½ cup grated parmesan cheese
    2 coddled eggs
    1 Maui onion cut into very thin rings
    croutons (recipe follows)

In a large wooden bowl, suitable for serving, mash garlic and anchovies against the inside surface of the bowl with a fork. Add mustard, pepper, lemon juice, olive oil, Worcestershire sauce and blend. Coddle eggs for 2 minutes in boiling water. Make the croutons.

Toss the greens and Maui onion in salad bowl until
all are glistening with dressing. Break in the coddled
eggs and toss to distribute throughout the salad.
Grate the cheese over all. Add croutons.

Serves 4 generous portions

Croutons:

1½ cups bread cubes (¾ to 1-inch square),
   French or whole wheat
¼ cup of olive oil (enough to just cover the pan)
2 cloves of garlic, minced
¼ cup Maui onion, minced

In a heavy frying pan, pour enough oil to cover
bottom. Begin heating on high while adding garlic
and onion. As onion and garlic begin to brown, add
bread cubes. Carefully toss to coat cubes. Heat until
the cubes are toasted, not burnt. Serve on salad or
with soup.

Seared Hawaiian Shutome on Chunky Tomato & Maui Onion Vinaigrette with Avacado Butter

Chef Roger Dikon suggests this as either a salad or a main course. Fresh fish, ripe tomatoes and just-picked herbs are the secret to duplicating this recipe as it would be served at the Prince Court in the Maui Prince Hotel.

4 pieces Hawaiian shutome (swordfish)
3 tablespoons olive oil or macadamia nut oil
1 teaspoon Hawaiian salt
1 teaspoon ground black pepper

Season and sear fish in oil in a very hot pan. Keep fish undercooked. Serve on a bed of Chunky Tomato & Maui Onion Vinaigrette. Drizzle Avocado Butter on top. (Recipes follow)

Serves 4

Sweet Onion Salads

Chunky Tomato & Maui Onion Vinaigrette:

2 large ripe tomatoes, diced
¼ cup Maui onion, minced
½ teaspoon garlic, minced
3 tablespoons balsamic vinegar
⅓ cup fresh chopped basil
2 tablespoons fresh herbs (suggested: cilantro, thyme, parsley)
Hawaiian salt and freshly ground pepper to taste
2 tablespoons virgin olive oil

Mix all ingredients together.

Makes 1½ to 2 cups

Avocado Butter:

1 whole ripe avocado
3 tablespoons lime juice
salt to taste
4 tablespoons (approximately) virgin olive oil

Blend all ingredients in a blender or food processor, adding oil and lime juice as needed.

Nori-Crusted Sashimi Salad with Poi Pesto

Dining at Avalon Restaurant in Lahaina is a memorable treat that keeps visitors and locals returning for more. Chef/owner Mark Ellman never stops finding new flavor combinations and creative presentations.

1 pound ahi steak (fresh tuna)
¼ cup macadamia nut oil
4 ounces furikake (nori or seasoned dried
    seaweed flakes)
1 tomato, sliced and marinated in pineapple rice
    vinegar, ginger, mint and shoyu (soy sauce)
½ pound mixed greens (preferably Kula greens)
1 Sharwil avocado
1 small Maui onion, sliced thinly

Roll ahi in macadamia nut oil then in furikake. Sear for five seconds on each side over very high heat. Set aside. Toss greens in marinade drained from the tomatoes. Divide greens into 4 equal portions and place in center of four large plates. Slice the avocado (lengthwise slices) and fan one quarter of the slices attractively on one side of each plate. Place onion and tomato slices on the opposite side of each plate.

Slice the seared ahi into ¼-inch slices and arrange over the salads.

Drizzle Poi Pesto over all. (Recipe follows.)

Serves 4

Poi Pesto:

8 ounces poi
4 ounces fresh, chopped ginger
4 ounces goat cheese
2 ounces roasted garlic
1 ounce chervil
1 cup mineral water
Hawaiian salt or kosher salt to taste
chile pepper water to taste

In a blender, starting with the poi, blend ingredients until puréed.

Avalon Ahi & Taro Salad

Chef Mark Ellman calls for some exotic ingredients in his poki-style salad...but then, that's what makes it uniquely his.

3 ounces sashimi-quality ahi (tuna), cubed
3 ounces cubed cooked taro
1 ounce Maui onion, julienned
½ teaspoon fresh chopped ginger
2 ounces shoyu (soy sauce)
½ teaspoon pure sesame oil
1 tablespoon chopped ogo (seaweed)
1 teaspoon chile pepper water
1 ounce toasted diced macadamia nuts
1 teaspoon toasted sesame seeds
1 tablespoon Cilantro Mac Nut Oil
   (recipe follows)
½ teaspoon tobiko (fish roe)

In a bowl combine the first 10 ingredients. Toss and let sit for 15 minutes. Mound the fish salad in center of a plate. Spoon Cilantro Mac Nut Oil around the salad. Sprinkle tobiko on top of salad. Serve with taro chips.

Cilantro Mac Nut Oil:

¼ cup macadamia nut oil
⅛ cup cilantro
salt
pepper, freshly ground

Put all ingredients in a blender and purée until
smooth.

Cafe Kula Spicy Black Bean Salad in a Tropical Farm Papaya

Chef Kathleen Daelemans was the first on Maui to feature healthy, low fat menus at Cafe Kula Restaurant.

- 1 quart cooked black beans
- 2 large sweet red tomatoes, diced
- 2 large sweet red peppers, diced
- 1 Maui onion, diced
- 2 bunches of cilantro
- 1 ounce Vietnamese chile paste
  or chopped jalapeño
- 2 ounces balsamic vinegar
- 1 ounce extra virgin olive oil
- 2 ripened tropical papayas

Gently, but thoroughly, combine beans, diced ingredients, cilantro, chile paste, vinegar and oil. Cut papayas in half lengthwise and scoop out seeds.* Spoon mounds of salad into each papaya half.

Serves 4 as a side dish or 2 as a luncheon entree

*Before filling papaya half, slice a thin strip of the peel away to 'flatten' the rounded bottom of the shell. This will keep it upright on the serving dish when filled.

MAUI ONION SOUPS

Award-Winning Maui Onion Gumbo

Chef Martina Hilldorfer loves showing off her style at events like the Maui Onion Festival at Whalers Village... that's where this soup won its award.

- 1 pound Portuguese sausage, diced
- 1 medium Maui onion, diced
- 2 stalks celery, diced
- 1 small green pepper, diced
- 1 medium tomato, diced
- 2 tablespoons tomato paste
- 1 quart fish stock or clam juice
- 12 crab claws, poached
- 12 shrimp, poached
- 16 scallops, poached
- 1 (15-ounce) can kidney beans
- 1 cup of okra, sliced
- 1 teaspoon ground cumin
- ¼ teaspoon ground allspice
- 1 tablespoon Cajun spice
- ½ teaspoon each basil, thyme and garlic
- 2 tablespoons olive oil
- ¼ cup brown roux* (enough to thicken)

Sauté sausage, onion, celery and green pepper until soft. Add tomatoes, tomato paste, fish stock and spices. Simmer 15 minutes. Add kidney beans and okra. Simmer 15 minutes. Add brown roux to thicken slightly. Garnish with poached shellfish.

Serves 4

* To make brown roux, mix ¼ cup flour and ¼ cup oil. Brown on low heat until chocolate-colored, 15 to 30 minutes.

Stella's French Onion Soup

The real woman behind Stella Blue's Cafe in Kihei is Janie Ennis. Her cooking is honest, the portions generous and the ingredients organic whenever possible.

4 cups thinly sliced Maui onions
4 tablespoons butter
6 cups beef bouillon
¼ cup dry white wine
6 slices toasted French bread
1½ cups fresh grated Parmesan or
    Swiss cheese
salt and pepper to taste

Sauté onions in heated butter until slightly browned. Pour in bouillon and bring to a boil. Reduce heat, cover and simmer 20 minutes. Add wine, salt and pepper. Simmer 10 minutes more. Pour into 6 oven-proof bowls or 1 large casserole. Top with toasted French bread and sprinkle generously with cheese. Bake in preheated oven at 350 degrees F for 20 minutes. Put under broiler until cheese is melted and crusty.

Serves 6

Loving Cup
Maui Onion Soup

Duane Kenward, like so many mainland transplants, finds he is eating healthier here on Maui. This is his 'lighter' version of Maui Onion soup...

4 Maui onions, sliced and cut in half
2 tablespoons margarine
2 tablespoons flour
1 (15-ounce) can low-salt beef broth
1 (15-ounce) can vegetable broth
½ cup red wine or sherry
1 cup whole wheat croutons
½ to 1 cup low-fat Swiss or Jack cheese,
   shredded

In a 2-quart saucepan, sauté onions in margarine just until transparent. Remove from heat and sprinkle with flour. Stir to coat onions. Continue to stir and add both cans of broth, a little at a time. Return to heat. Simmer 5 to 10 minutes. Add wine and heat for 2 minutes—be careful not to bring to a boil.

Ladle soup into oven-proof bowls, top with croutons, then cheese. Slip under broiler for a few minutes until the cheese is bubbling and just starting to brown. Serve immediately.

Serves 4

Creamy Maui Onion Soup with Fresh Chives

Chef Steve Amaral often serves up creamy soups like this overlooking the pool at the Kea Lani Hotel in Wailea.

  4 Maui onions, diced
  1 ounce minced garlic
  2 tablespoons butter
  1 cup dry sherry
  1½ quarts chicken or vegetable broth
  1 bouquet garni of fresh herbs
  4 ounces blonde roux
      (2 ounces of butter plus 2 ounces of flour)
  8 ounces heavy cream
  salt and ground white pepper to taste
  1 bunch chives, minced

Heat 2 tablespoons of butter in heavy 2-quart soup pot. Sauté Maui onion and garlic until translucent. Deglaze pan with sherry. Add broth and bouquet garni to pot. Simmer 30 minutes.

Prepare blonde roux by blending flour into heated butter in a non-aluminum pot and gently heating for 30 minutes. Whisk roux into the broth. Cook another 30 minutes. Skim and stir frequently. Add cream slowly while whisking soup. Add salt and ground white pepper to taste. Pour hot soup into a blender and process until smooth. Add minced chives and serve while soup is still hot.

Serves 4

Maui Onion Gazpacho

When a friend asked for this recipe, I was surprised. I thought it was nothing special. Was it the soup or because we ate it on my lanai late one perfect afternoon after a day at the beach? In any case, no one would guess it is so easy to make!

1 Maui onion
1 green pepper, seeded
1 cucumber, peeled
1 ripe tomato, seeded, peeled and chopped
1 clove garlic, minced (optional)
½ small lemon, juiced
sprig of dill weed, chopped, or pinch of
    dill seed
3 cups spicy tomato juice or V-8

Cut Maui onion and green pepper into chunks. Place in food processor bowl with minced garlic. Pulse until roughly chopped. Add cucumber chunks and tomato on top of the chopped vegetables in the processor bowl. Pour lemon juice over all, add dill. Pulse again until well chopped. In a large serving bowl, blend chopped vegetable mixture into the tomato juice. If all ingredients were cold, the soup is ready. Otherwise, chill well. (Chill quickly in the freezer, but don't freeze the soup,

44

to keep flavors distinct and fresh. Chilling overnight is easier and allows the flavors to blend.) Garnish suggestions: sour cream, chives, croutons, nasturtiums or other edible flowers or fresh herbs.

Makes 4 to 5 cups

Osso Bucco, La Pasteria Style

La Pasteria is a small bistro-style restaurant in a Kihei shopping center that also makes fresh pasta for many restaurants around Maui.

> 5 pounds veal shanks, cut into 1½ to 2-inch pieces
> 2 Maui onions, diced
> 4 carrots, grated
> 2 stalks celery
> 2 pounds sliced mushrooms
> 2 cups sherry
> 4 cups veal stock or light beef broth
> bouquet garni of fresh parsley, basil and oregano
> salt and freshly ground pepper to taste

Put all ingredients in a large soup pot. Bring to simmer and reduce, reduce, reduce! Chef Ron Mazzoncini recommends simmering to reduce the soup for at least 9 hours.

Serves 4

Maui Onion Soups

MAINLY ONIONS FOR DINNER

Chicken & Maui Onion in a Clay Pot

Chef Martina Hilldorfer racked up the highest number of points in the Maui Onion Festival Recipe Contest with this recipe. She created a clay 'onion' that you must crack open with a mallet! If you'd rather not get violent with your food, you can cook the dish in a terra-cotta baking dish.

2 (8-ounce) boneless chicken breasts,
    cut in half
salt and freshly ground pepper to taste
1 ounce butter
2 shallots, diced
2 ounces white wine
2 ounces strong chicken stock
1 pinch saffron
1 cup heavy cream
4 small Maui onions, peeled and
    hollowed out
1 red bell pepper, julienned
8 ti leaves, stemmed and lightly blanched
2 pounds lead-free, low fire clay

Season the chicken with salt and freshly ground pepper. In a hot sauté pan, add butter and chicken. Cook until almost done and nicely browned. Remove chicken. Add shallots to pan and deglaze with wine. Add chicken stock. Reduce until almost dry. Add saffron and heavy cream, reduce by half.

Place the chicken inside the hollow onions. Fill each with cream sauce. Place some red bell pepper on top of each. Place each onion in the center of 2 ti leaves laid in an X. Gather up the sides of the leaves like a lau lau. Secure the bundle by wrapping the end of one of the leaves around the rest just above the onion.

Roll out clay using heavy plastic wrap between the clay and rolling pin. Place each bundle on a 10 x 10 x ¼-inch sheet of clay. Fold clay over the bundle just to cover the onion, leaving the tops of the ti leaves exposed. It should resemble a brown onion with green leaves. Prick a small hole in the top to allow steam to escape. Bake at 250 degrees F for 40 to 60 minutes. Crack each bundle open with a mallet.

Serves 4

Steamed Papio On Warm Maui Onion Marmalade

Chef Roger Dikon says this ultra-simple fish dish can be garnished with Lychee Salsa and Ocean Greens (seaweed). It's delicious even if you can't find these exotic ingredients.

4 filets of papio, 6 ounces
1 pound mixed salad greens
Hawaiian salt to taste
Maui Onion Marmalade (recipe follows)

Steam fish in large sauté pan or wok until the meat flakes off, approximately 5 to 8 minutes. Remove and keep warm.

Add greens to the pan, tossing until wilted. Season with Hawaiian salt.

Serve fish with Warm Maui Onion Marmalade. Garnish with greens.

Serves 4

Warm Maui Onion Marmalade:

3 cups Maui onion, sliced
2 tablespoons olive oil
1 cup heavy cream
¼ teaspoon fresh thyme
¼ teaspoon Hawaiian salt or sea salt

In a large sauté pan on medium heat, add oil then onions. Sauté slowly, letting them caramelize. After 10 minutes, add thyme and salt. Turn heat to low for another 10 minutes.

Meanwhile, reduce cream down to ¾ cup in a heavy-bottomed sauce pan. Add it to the pan with the caramelized onion and mix. Cook for 3 minutes.

Black Bean & Maui Onion Chile

Chris and Becky Speer's Pauwela Cafe in the Haiku Cannery is a great place to grab a Kalua turkey sandwich or this great chili on the way to Hana.

3 pounds top round beef, cut into ½-inch cubes
2 Maui onions, chopped
2 bell peppers, chopped
6 cloves of garlic
¼ cup chile powder
2 teaspoons cumin
2 teaspoons oregano
4 cups tomato sauce
6 cups cooked black beans
salt and black pepper to taste
3 tablespoons olive oil

Heat oil in a large skillet. Sear beef cubes on high heat. Reduce heat and add onion, peppers and garlic. Add chile powder, cumin and oregano. Sauté with beef and vegetables. Cook 10 minutes. Add tomato sauce and black beans. Simmer chile at least 1 hour. Add salt and pepper to taste.

Serve with sour cream, salsa, brown rice and tortilla chips for a meal.

Serves 6 generously.

Maui Burger

1½ pounds fresh ground beef
1 large Maui onion, sliced
1 tomato, sliced
garlic salt and pepper for seasoning
1 pound round loaf of Portuguese sweet bread,
    or any round loaf of bread

Shape the ground beef into one large hamburger patty. Season with garlic salt and pepper to taste. *Be sure the patty is no thicker than the usual size patty.* Grill over medium coals on a charcoal grill, or in a very large skillet, until juices run clear from the middle of the patty. Slice the loaf of sweet bread in half horizontally so it resembles one large hamburger bun. Place cooked burger on bottom half of the 'bun' and arrange sliced tomato and onion on top. Replace the top of the bun. Slice into 4 wedge-shaped sandwiches.

Serves 4

The sweet bread makes the Maui Burger into something really special. Most quick-stop places on the island sell 'red' hot dogs in sweet bread rolls and they are a local favorite, too.

Stuffed Maui Onion Bread

Chef Robert O'Brien of The Westin Maui created this recipe. If time is too short to make your own bread, the onion and crab filling can be stuffed into a loaf of French bread or used as a topping for a plain pizza crust.

3 to 3½ cups all-purpose flour
1½ tablespoons sugar
1 tablespoon shortening
1 package dry yeast
1⅛ cups warm water (120 to 130 degrees F)
2 tablespoons dehydrated Maui onion

To dehydrate the Maui onion: Place 2 cups of chopped onion into a dehydrator or on a very low temperature in the oven. Do not brown.

For the Bread: Mix 2 cups of the flour with sugar, shortening, dehydrated Maui onion, and yeast in a 3-quart bowl. Add warm water. Mix on low speed for 1 minute, scraping frequently. Mix on medium speed for 1 minute more. Stir in enough of the remaining flour to make the dough easy to handle. Turn dough onto lightly floured surface, knead until elastic. Place in a greased bowl, turn greased-side up. Cover and let rise in a warm place until double (40 to 60 minutes). Punch down and divide

in half. Let rest 5 minutes. Roll halves into balls,
rolling in some of the leftover dehydrated onions.
Let rise until double. Bake at 425 degrees F for
20 to 30 minutes. Remove and cool on wire racks.

Filling:

½ cup washed, roughly chopped spinach
4 ounces cream cheese
¼ to ½ cup sour cream
4 ounces goat cheese
1 teaspoon fresh garlic, minced
¼ cup Maui onion, diced
½ cup crab, broken and drained
¼ cup water chestnuts, julienned
salt and pepper to taste

Wilt spinach in a sauté pan. Drain and chop. Fold
softened cream cheese into sour cream. Crumble in
the goat cheese. Add garlic and fresh Maui onion.
Mix well. Salt and pepper to taste. Fold in the crab
and water chestnuts. Cut out the top of the bread
and hollow out the insides. Stuff filling into the
bread. Lightly toast whole filled bread (and inside
pieces) in hot oven.

Maui Onion & Smoked Duck Lasagna

Shannon Crivello entered this recipe in the 1994 Maui Onion Festival. If you don't have duck, try leftover turkey cooked on a Weber grill!

1 batch of Maui Onion Pasta dough,
   (See page 76) rolled in sheets
1 shallot bulb, sliced
1 tablespoon oregano
1 tablespoon thyme
1 tablespoon basil
1 clove garlic
1 tablespoon olive oil
2 cups white wine
4 small Maui onions, puréed
6 golden tomatoes, puréed
1 yellow bell pepper, puréed
1 cup sugar
salt and freshly ground pepper to taste
1 red bell pepper, diced
1 green bell pepper, diced

Combine shallots, oregano, basil, thyme and garlic and brown in olive oil. Deglaze pan with wine. In a saucepan add this mixture to puréed onion, tomatoes and sugar. Season to taste. Simmer for ½ hour.

Filling Ingredients:

1 breast of smoked duck, shredded
1 cup shitake mushrooms, finely chopped
1 cup olives, chopped
½ cup Maui onion, chopped
1 tablespoon garlic, minced
1 (6-ounce) can tomato paste
8 sun-dried tomatoes
1 cup spinach, cooked and drained
1 cup ricotta cheese

Combine all filling ingredients except for sun-dried tomatoes, cheese and spinach. Sauté all until lightly cooked. Remove from heat and combine last three ingredients into mixture. Spoon filling between layers of lasagna noodles in a 9 x 13-inch baking pan. Bake 10 to 20 minutes at 375 degrees F.

Generously spoon sauce on plate and serve lasagna on top. Garnish with diced red and green peppers.

Serves 6

Three-Way Maui Carnitas

Rich Santos says: Choose one meat or make a batch of each for a large gathering.

1 pound beef or pork, cubed
or 3 boneless, skinless chicken breasts, cubed
1 bell pepper, thinly sliced
1 small Maui onion, thinly sliced
12 tortillas (corn or flour)
1 Maui onion, minced
2 cloves garlic
1/4 cup fresh cilantro, chopped
1/4 cup fresh basil, chopped
1 tablespoon oregano
12 ounces green taco sauce
16 ounces orange juice
1 tablespoon lime juice
1 tablespoon canola oil
1 bell pepper, cubed

Heat oil in skillet. Brown the meat, then add minced Maui onion and garlic in same skillet. When all is browned, add cilantro, basil and oregano. Add green taco sauce, orange juice and pepper cubes. Cover, reduce heat to low. Simmer about 1 hour to reduce liquid by nearly half.

Serve carnitas rolled up in warm tortillas with thinly sliced bell pepper and Maui onion.

Serves 6

Tropical Green Papaya Chicken

Joanna Jeronimo swears the inspiration for this dish was the fragrant bush (rosemary) in her yard…and she wasn't even sure which herb it was when she started experimenting.

    4 skinless, boneless chicken breast halves
    seasoning (see below)
    1 large green papaya
    1 medium Maui onion
    1 ounce chicken broth or white wine
    2 teaspoons fresh rosemary
    1 teaspoon each: fresh thyme, fresh basil and
        dried Italian herbs
    1 (2-ounce) jar pimientos
    2 ounces slivered almonds
    fresh chopped parsley for garnish

Seasoning: Combine ½ teaspoon salt, ½ teaspoon coarse white pepper, 1 teaspoon orange zest, ½ teaspoon onion powder, ¼ teaspoon garlic powder, a pinch of cayenne pepper, and a pinch of celery salt.

Rub seasoning on both sides of chicken breasts. Place in a 9 x 12-inch baking dish. Peel papaya and cut in half lengthwise. Remove seeds, and cut into slices. Arrange in dish, alternating chicken and papaya slices. Slice Maui onion into ¼-inch slices. Separate into rings and arrange attractively over the chicken. Add liquid without disturbing seasoning. Sprinkle with herbs. Cover with foil and bake at 375 degrees F for 45 minutes or until chicken is no longer pink and papaya is tender. Remove cover.

Sprinkle drained pimientos and almonds over chicken. Broil for 2 minutes or until chicken is browned. Garnish with parsley.

Serves 4

Big Eye Ahi Tuna & Maui Onion Confit

Chef Darren McGraw is young, talented, and has developed a following from his work at the Five Palms Grill in Kihei. Try this simple yet elegant cold dish.

    6 ounces big eye ahi (tuna)
    4 ounces clarified butter
    1 cup chopped Maui onions

    2 ounces (handful) baby Savoy spinach
    ½ ounce vinaigrette (recipe follows)
    12 French green beans
    4 baby yellow wax potatoes, sliced

In a cold sauté pan, braise ahi in butter until rare. Add onions and continue to cook on low. When ahi is almost done, remove from pan. Leave onions to braise to a marmalade consistency. Allow both to cool to room temperature. Chill.

Meanwhile, toss spinach in vinaigrette. Separately toss potatoes and beans. Arrange neatly on sides of plate with spinach in the middle. Garnish with fried onion (recipe follows).

Serves 2

Vinaigrette:

½ ounce balsamic vinegar
3 sprigs fresh thyme
1 shallot
1 clove garlic
1 teaspoon Dijon mustard
1 ounce extra virgin olive oil

In a blender, add ingredients one at a time. Olive oil should be last. You may add salt and pepper to taste.

Fried Onion Garnish:

¼ Maui onion, sliced
flour
canola oil

Dip onion in flour. Fry in canola oil, then drain.

VEGETABLE DISHES STARRING MAUI ONION

Sweet Potato Cakes

Chef James McDonald serves fabulous food at his beach front restaurant Pacific O in Lahaina.

> 1 large sweet potato, grated
> 1½ ounces Maui onion, grated
> 2 tablespoons green onion, chopped
> 1 egg
> ½ ounce flour
> ¾ teaspoon salt
> dash white pepper
> 1 teaspoon Chinese parsley, chopped
> ½ teaspoon lemon juice
> 1 cup Hawaiian macadamia nut oil
>   or canola oil

Combine all ingredients except oil. Form into pan-cake-sized patties. In a large skillet, pan-fry pancakes in oil over medium heat until lightly browned and heated thoroughly. Serve with sour cream, if desired.

2 to 4 servings

Maui Onion Soufflé with Red Pepper Sabayon

Randall Bouck wowed them during the professional competition at the first Maui County Ag Trade Show & Sampling.

1 stick butter
3 medium Maui onions, chopped fine
1½ cups all-purpose flour
2 cups milk
1 tablespoon mixed herbs, chopped fine
1 teaspoon Hawaiian or kosher salt
pinch of black pepper
5 egg yolks
5 egg whites
1 tablespoon sugar

Melt 1 tablespoon of the butter in a sauté pan. Sauté onions, stirring occasionally, until moisture evaporates and onions are golden. Set aside. Melt remaining butter in a saucepan and add flour, whisking constantly. Cook 2 to 3 minutes, but do not brown. Remove pan from heat and whisk in the milk. Return pan to the heat and continue to whisk until mixture is thick and pulls away from side of pan. Mix in sautéed onions, herbs, salt and pepper. Cool. Incorporate egg yolks slowly.

Preheat oven to 375 degrees F. In electric mixer with whipping attachment, whip egg whites and sugar together until they resemble soft peaks. Mix one quarter of the beaten egg whites into the batter, then fold in remaining whites, a third at a time. Butter and flour 8 soufflé cups. Spoon mixture into cups and bake for 35 minutes, until puffed and brown. Serve immediately after making an incision on top of each soufflé and spooning in some Red Pepper Sabayon.

Makes 8 soufflés

Red Pepper Sabayon:

2 roasted red bell peppers, peeled and seeded
1 ripe tomato, peeled and seeded
1 tablespoon white vinegar
½ cup extra virgin olive oil
1 tablespoon Hawaiian or kosher salt
pinch fresh ground black pepper

In blender, purée peppers, tomato and vinegar until well blended. Drizzle in olive oil. Season with salt and pepper.

Makes about 1 cup

Maui Onion & Potato Pie

Veronica Stallard wins every time she enters a local cooking competition. This was her entry in the '95 Maui County Ag Trade Show & Sampling at Tedeschi Winery.

Potato Crust:

2 large potatoes, finely grated
1 large Maui onion, finely grated
1 egg, slightly beaten
1/8 teaspoon salt
dash of cayenne
black pepper to taste

Mix all ingredients. Press into and up the sides of a 9-inch pie plate. Pat with paper towel to soak up excess moisture. Bake crust at 375 degrees F for 20 minutes until lightly browned.

Filling:

4 large or 5 medium Maui onions, thinly sliced
2 tablespoons olive oil
1 tablespoon butter
2 eggs, beaten
1 cup evaporated milk (skim or regular)
2 tablespoons flour
½ teaspoon salt
½ teaspoon Cajun spice
¼ teaspoon black pepper
¼ teaspoon garlic powder or minced fresh garlic
2½ ounces grated Gruyère or Swiss cheese
1 red pepper, thinly sliced

Sauté the onions in olive oil and butter until lightly
browned. Combine eggs, evaporated milk, flour,
salt, Cajun spice, pepper and garlic in a large bowl.
Add sautéed onions and 1 ounce of the cheese.
Pour into crust. Sprinkle remaining cheese and
arrange red pepper slices in a pinwheel design on top
of the pie. Bake at 375 degrees F for 30 minutes or
until browned.

Serves 4 to 6

Fried Maui Onions

Chef Becky Speere has a knack for zapping local foods with Mainland appeal. These crunchy onions are great over seared fish or as a side dish for poki.

5 cups peanut oil
2 large Maui onions, thinly sliced
1 cup all purpose flour
1 teaspoon paprika
1 teaspoon salt
1 teaspoon black pepper
½ teaspoon cayenne pepper

Heat oil to 350 degrees F. Mix all dry ingredients together to blend. Toss in the onions to coat. Fry onions in oil until crisp and golden brown. Drain on paper towel.

Makes 4 servings

Plantation House Cheddar Cheese Scalloped Tatters

Chef Alex Stanislaw was caught grilling the meat for his entry at the "Ulupalakua Thing" in the parking lot on a tiny Weber while smoking a big cigar.

    4 potatoes, sliced ⅛-inch thick
    1 clove garlic
    1 cup heavy cream
    1 teaspoon garlic powder
    salt and freshly ground pepper to taste
    ½ pound extra sharp cheddar cheese, grated
    1 Maui onion, sliced paper thin
    1 teaspoon olive oil

Rinse sliced potatoes. Rub the garlic clove over the entire inside of an oven-proof casserole. Mix garlic powder in cream. Cover bottom of casserole with a layer of potato. Salt potatoes, then cover with a layer of onion and cheese. Repeat. Continue to layer, finishing with cheese. Pour in cream to just below the top layer. Cover with foil. Bake at 375 degrees F for 45 to 55 minutes. Remove foil for last 10 minutes for a crust.

Makes 6 servings

Dilled Maui Onions

Paulette DeMaestre left the corporate world to relax the rest of her life away on Maui. Ha! She is one of the busiest people on the island.

3 or 4 large Maui onions, thinly sliced
1 crisp cucumber, thinly sliced
1 teaspoon dill
1 teaspoon sugar
1 cup white vinegar
½ cup water
salt and freshly ground pepper to taste

Mix all ingredients, except onion and cucumber in a shallow glass or ceramic dish with a wooden spoon. Add cucumber and onion. Toss until well coated. Season to taste with salt and freshly ground pepper. Let marinate 1 to 3 hours before serving. Refrigerate any unused portion.

Makes 6 servings

Oignon avec Vin de Xérès

A hearty vegetable dish that includes all the favorite onion soup ingredients... but cooks up like a casserole. Paulette DeMaestre says it's a family favorite.

6 to 8 Maui onions, sliced about ¼-inch thick
6 tablespoons real butter
3 tablespoons cornstarch
1 cup plus 3 tablespoons chicken broth, ice cold
freshly ground pepper to taste
⅓ cup dry sherry
2 cups small croutons
5 tablespoons melted butter
1½ cups fresh, coarsely chopped or grated
    Gruyère or Swiss cheese
5 tablespoons finely grated Romano cheese

Sauté onions in 6 tablespoons of butter until barely tender. Combine cornstarch and chicken broth, add to onion mixture. Add pepper and stir in sherry. Cook and stir over low heat until thickened and bubbly. Pour mixture into large, shallow baking dish. Toss 5 tablespoons of the melted butter with croutons and spoon over the onion mixture in pan. Cover with the cheeses and broil approximately 1 minute until the cheese melts.

Serves 6

Haiku Mushroom Ragout & Red-Glazed Maui Onions

Chef Chris Speere suggests this combo as a saucy side dish for most any meat... or try it over wild rice.

> 1 Maui onion, minced
> 2 cloves garlic, minced
> 4 ounces butter
> 1 pound whole Haiku mushrooms
>   (or sliced if larger variety is used)
> 2 ounces lemon juice
> 4 ounces white wine
> 2 tablespoons parsley, minced
> 2 ounces chicken stock
> 8 ounces cream
> salt and freshly ground pepper to taste

In heavy skillet over medium-high heat, sauté onions and garlic in butter. Push aside, add mushrooms and quickly sauté. Remove mushrooms. Add remaining ingredients and reduce until slightly thickened. Add mushrooms back to ragout and season to taste with salt and freshly ground pepper.

Makes 4 servings, or about 3 cups

Red-Glazed Maui Onions:

1 large Maui onion, sliced
8 ounces red wine (Tedeschi Plantation Red)
2 ounces sugar (Maui brand raw sugar)

Method: Combine all ingredients in a pan. Cook until onions are tender and the wine forms a thick glaze.

Makes about 2 cups

Long lines form at the official Maui Onion Ring station at events like the Maui Onion Festival and the Ulupalakua Thing. Want to know the secret ingredients for these golden rings? It's fresh sliced Maui onion, an ancient three-foot wide wok blackened with frequent use and Krustez batter mix!

Maui Onion Pasta

Chef Shannon Crivello's speedy adaptation of the hand-mixed version.

>   1 pound bread flour
>   5 eggs
>   ½ ounce olive oil
>   1 cup puréed Maui onions

Combine flour, eggs, olive oil and pureed onion (add a dash of salt if desired) in a food processor. Pulse ingredients just until well integrated. Let rest 5 minutes.

Roll out on a floured board with a rolling pin or use a pasta machine. Cut dough into preferred width of noodle… or use in sheets for lasagna.

Makes 1¼ pounds pasta dough

No Ka Oi
Maui Onion Soufflé

Kay Sinnett, of the northwest chain of Sinnett's Markets fame, is a snowbird who winters on Maui. She won the very first Maui Onion Festival Cooking Contest with this recipe.

- 2 large Maui onions, chopped
- 2 cups shredded cheese
- 1¾ cups real mayonnaise
- ¼ teaspoon Tiger Sauce
- ¼ teaspoon Worcestershire sauce
- 1 (8-ounce) can water chestnuts, chopped

Combine all ingredients in an oven-proof dish. Bake at 375 degrees F for 25 to 30 minutes. Serve with crackers.

Serves 4 as a side dish

LUNCH FAVORITES AND SIDE DISHES

Plate Lunch Hamburger Gravy with Zucchini

Bonnie Tuell is co-owner and executive chef for the Maui Jelly Factory. The Wailuku-based processing plant produces tropical jams, sauces and syrups that are distributed globally under the Jelly Factory label and various private labels, including Hilo Hattie and Liberty House.

    ¼ cup bacon, chopped
    1 pound ground beef
    1 medium Maui onion, chopped
    1 tablespoon shoyu (soy sauce)
    1½ teaspoons salt
    ½ teaspoon sugar
    3 medium-sized zucchini, sliced ¼-inch thick
    2 tablespoons all-purpose flour
    1 cup warm water

In a large skillet, sauté bacon slightly. Do not drain fat. Add ground beef and Maui onion. Cook until hamburger is almost done. Add seasonings and zucchini. Simmer until zucchini is tender. Combine flour and water for gravy, then add to the simmering skillet ingredients. Continue to simmer until gravy thickens.

Serve with or over rice… preferably in a styrofoam tray with individual shoyu packets!

Serves 4

Korean Style Beef

This recipe was featured in a Maui County Farm Bureau pamphlet. Serve with, what else—two scoops rice and kim chee!

1½ pounds bean sprouts
½ pound cucumbers, shredded
½ pound daikon (Chinese radish), shredded
1 clove garlic, crushed
1½ pounds boneless sirloin beef, sliced thin
½ pound Maui onion, in ½-inch pieces
½ pound bell pepper, in ½-inch pieces
¼ cup green onion, in ½-inch pieces
salt to taste
1 tablespoon sesame seeds
sesame oil

Sauce: Mix together 2 teaspoons Korean red pepper sauce, 1 cup soy sauce, ½ cup honey. Let stand during preparation of dish.

Blanch sprouts, cucumber and daikon in hot, salted water. Drain and arrange on serving platter. Preheat wok on high heat and coat with sesame oil. When oil is hot, add garlic and stir-fry. Remove before garlic burns. Stir-fry beef until rare, about 1 minute. Add salt if desired. Push beef to one side. Add Maui onions, peppers and green onion. Stir-fry until tender crisp, about 2 minutes. Gently toss vegetables with beef. Pour sauce over all, sprinkle with sesame seeds. Serve over bed of blanched vegetables.

Serves 4 to 5

Kalua Pork Buns

Rich Santos won the 1992 'Local Grinds Contest' for this entry, a variation on the local favorite called manapua.

1 (¼-ounce) package yeast
1¾ cups warm water
¾ cup sugar
1 teaspoon baking powder
6½ cups unsifted all-purpose flour

Dissolve yeast in warm water with sugar. Mix in baking powder and flour. Dough will be quite dry. Knead for 20 minutes until dough becomes smooth and elastic. Place in mixing bowl, cover with a damp cloth until dough doubles (about 3 hours.) Punch down and knead again for 5 minutes. Dough is now ready.

Filling:

4 cups leftover kalua pork
   (see page 90)
1 small Maui onion, diced
4 tablespoons catsup
2 tablespoons hoisin sauce
1 tablespoon dark soy sauce
2 tablespoons honey
2 tablespoons oyster sauce

Combine all ingredients and mix thoroughly.

Divide dough into 24 balls. Flatten into 4-inch circles leaving the center twice as thick as the sides. Place 1 tablespoon of filling in the center of each dough circle. Gather up the sides around the filling. Twist firmly to seal. Place on a 2-inch square of waxed paper, twist-side down. Allow 2 inches between buns on baking sheet, allow to rise for 1 hour. No need to remove wax paper at this point.

Steam buns for 15 minutes in a bamboo or metal steamer—*or*—brush buns with an egg wash (1 egg white, 1 teaspoon of water and ¼-teaspoon of sugar), then bake at 350 degree F for 20 to 25 minutes. Brush lightly with melted butter after removing from oven. Remove waxed paper just before eating.

Makes 24 buns

Pauwela Cafe Ahi Poki

If you like sashimi (raw fish), you'll understand why poki is an island favorite. Becky Speere's version has a bit more vegetable than the usual poki.

1½ cups lemon juice
2 pounds ahi (tuna), diced ¾-inch pieces
4 cucumbers, diced ¾-inch pieces
6 tomatoes, diced ¾-inch pieces
2 Maui onions, diced ½-inch pieces
½ cup capers, drained
½ cup extra virgin olive oil
4 teaspoons Hawaiian or kosher salt
½ teaspoon black pepper
1 tablespoon dried oregano
1 teaspoon ground cumin
1 teaspoon Hawaiian chile paste
(recipe follows)

Marinate the diced ahi in lemon juice overnight. Add in remaining ingredients, and mix well. Serve with an assortment of fresh mixed lettuces and fried taro chips.

Serves 12

Hawaiian Chili Paste:

Mix together:
1 cup fresh red Hawaiian chile purée
⅓ cup wine vinegar
3 teaspoons chopped garlic
1 teaspoon salt
1 tablespoon fish sauce (patis)

Makes 12 servings

Pauwela Cafe
Seared Opah Poki

Chris Speere has his own version of poki. This one uses opah, also called moonfish.

1 pound opah, diced ½-inch pieces
½ cup lemon juice
½ cup lime juice
2 ounces sake
3 tablespoons shoyu (soy sauce)
1 ounce olive oil
2 tablespoons salt
2 tablespoons cracked white peppercorns
½ cup chopped green onions
1 tomato, seeded and chopped
1 Maui onion, sliced
½ teaspoon ginger, chopped
½ teaspoon garlic, chopped
½ teaspoon red chile flakes

Marinate diced opah in first 8 ingredients overnight. Drain, add remaining ingredients. Mix well. In a hot wok or sauté pan, quickly sear the fish mixture. Serve with fried Maui onions and spicy Korean sauce.

Serves 4

Lunch Favorites and Side Dishes

Spicy Korean Sauce:

1 cup shoyu (soy sauce)
1 cup water
½ cup brown sugar
⅓ cup toasted sesame seeds
⅓ cup sweet chile sauce
1 teaspoon sesame oil
½ cup chopped green onions
1 tablespoon chopped cilantro

Combine first 6 ingredients in blender until smooth.

Add green onion and cilantro. Serve on Seared Opah Poki.

Makes 4 servings

Maui Onion Eggroll (Lumpia)

Chef Joe Balinbin shows off his extensive knowledge of ethnic cooking styles at the Kaanapali Beach Hotel. This recipe is a variation of the Chinese eggroll and Filipino lumpia.

8 ounces boneless chicken breast, julienned
2 tablespoons peanut oil
1 teaspoon ginger, minced
½ teaspoon garlic, minced
¼ cup sherry wine
¼ cup oyster sauce
1 pound Maui onions, julienned
¼ pound Shitake mushrooms, julienned
¼ pound celery, julienned
¼ pound carrots, julienned
¼ pound string beans, julienned
¼ pound bean sprouts
¼ pound watercress
14 lumpia or eggroll wrappers

Sauté chicken in peanut oil on medium-high heat. Add ginger, garlic, sherry and oyster sauce. Add julienned vegetables and stir-fry until tender. Cool in refrigerator. Place mixture in centers of lumpia wrappers, wrap two opposite sides over filling, then roll loosly. Moisten edges with egg whites. Deep-fry in oil until golden brown.

Makes 14 rolls

Easy Kalua Pork

This is a variation on the meat traditionally cooked in an underground imu and served with rice, poi, sweet potatoes, lomi lomi salmon and cabbage at luaus.

1 pork butt, 3 to 3½ pounds
1 tablespoon liquid smoke
¾ tablespoon Hawaiian, kosher or sea salt
ti leaves or cabbage leaves
1 head of cabbage, quartered

Place pork butt on aluminum foil sheet (large enough to wrap easily around the meat) inside a roasting pan. Pour liquid smoke over meat, sprinkle with salt. Place leaves around meat to keep it extra juicy. Wrap the meat with the first sheet of aluminum foil, trapping the seasonings inside. Repeat wrapping with two more sheets in alternating directions until fully covered on all sides. Place on rack in the roasting pan and fill the pan half full of water. Roast at 300 degrees F for at least 6 hours. Optional: Add cabbage to the pan so that it cooks for at least 1½ hours.

Shred the meat when done and just cool enough to handle. Pour some of the pan juices over the meat in a serving bowl to keep it juicy.

Serves 6 (Feeds more at a luau with all the side dishes!)

Flank Steak Ulupalakua Thing Poki

Chef Roger Dikon regularly creates this award-winning dish with seared beef and even venison.

- 1 pound flank steak, trimmed and peeled
- 1½ cup teriyaki sauce
- 1 medium Maui onion, julienned
- 1 large vine-ripened tomato
- 1 tablespoon chopped garlic
- 2 tablespoons chopped fresh ginger
- 1 tablespoon roasted kukui nut
- 1 tablespoon dark sesame oil
- 1 tablespoon chile paste or Hawaiian chile peppers to taste
- ½ cup green onion, cut into ½-inch lengths

Marinate flank steak in teriyaki sauce for 2 hours. Remove steak and broil over hot coals (preferably kiawe charcoal), 4 minutes per side. Meat should be rare to medium-rare inside. Slice across the bias. Slice again into thin pieces about the size of a quarter. Mix with the remaining ingredients.

Serves 4 as an appetizer

Tai Ching
Look Fun Noodles

Gertie Ching Ceballos enters almost every cooking contest on Maui and usually wins. Look Fun noodles are found in island supermarket cold cases (like fresh pasta) or packaged dried (like Top Ramen) in oriental food sections.

½ pound fresh Chinese peas
2 stalks celery, sliced diagonally
2 large Maui onions, diced
2 carrots, cut into shoestring strips
1 tablespoon corn oil
2 packages Look Fun noodles,
fresh (preferred) or dried (cooked to
    package directions)
1 pound cooked char siu, sliced (Chinese
    roast pork)
2 packages mung bean sprouts
6 green onions, sliced in 1 inch pieces
Chinese parsley sprigs for garnish

Seasoning: 2 tablespoons oyster sauce plus ¼ teaspoon black or white pepper

Quickly stir fry the Chinese peas, celery, Maui onion and carrots in hot oil. Add noodles. Add seasoning mixture and char siu pork, stir fry for an additional 2 minutes. Remove from heat, add bean sprouts and green onions. Toss lightly and garnish with snipped Chinese parsley.

Serves 4

Note: To serve this Maui style, load the noodles into a paper cone and eat with chopsticks.

A Maui onion should be enjoyed promptly after purchase. Their unusually high moisture content means they won't keep nearly as long as other types of onion.

Pickled Maui Onions with Ginger

Pickled vegetables are very popular in Hawaii, especially kim chee, tsukimono, or pickled Maui onion. Try some in place of a green salad.

    1½ pounds small Maui onions
    ¼ cup minced fresh ginger
    2 Hawaiian peppers, finely chopped
        or 1 teaspoon red pepper flakes
    1 cup cider vinegar
    ½ cup water
    1 tablespoon sugar
    2 teaspoons Hawaiian, kosher or sea salt

Peel onions. Cut in half or quarters. Place onions in a quart jar. Add ginger, red peppers, vinegar, water, sugar and salt. Cover jar and shake well. Refrigerate for 2 or 3 days, shaking the jar at least once a day.

Makes 1 quart

Maui Onion Sources:

Maui Jelly Factory
1-800-803-8343

• For Maui Onion Jelly, Maui Onion Mustard,
Maui Onion Jelly Gift Baskets

SANTOS! Products
(808)875-0457   Fax (808) 879-1283
116 Mehani Place, Kihei, Maui, HI 96753

• For Maui Onion Cookbook Gift Packs with the
exotic ingredients called for in these recipes

• Free calendar of Maui food events

Where to get Maui Onions
if you are on the Mainland:

Maui Produce Exchange
(510) 676-6284
391 Taylor Boulevard, Suite 105
Pleasant Hills, CA 94523

• Call first and they may be able to tell you of a
market in your area that carries the Kula Maui Onion

Maui onions can be taken to the mainland with passengers on airlines. As long as they are unblemished and insect-free, it doesn't matter if you bought them at a Farmers Market or the Kahului Safeway.

Remember: They must go through the Agricultural Station where baggage is screened.